ECHOES ACROSS A THOUSAND HILLS

For Judith,
echoing the future —
and the "thousand"
hills and valleys — all of
this! — from
Selwa, 4-1-95

ECHOES ACROSS A THOUSAND HILLS

AMELIA BLOSSOM PEGRAM

VISUAL RESPONSES
by **SELMA WALDMAN**

For:
Judith
the dance goes on...
Amelia Blossom Pegram
April '95

Africa World Press, Inc.
P.O. Box 1892
Trenton, New Jersey 08607

Africa World Press, Inc.

P. O. Box 1892
Trenton, NJ 08607

First Printing

Cover Design by Carles J. Juzang
Cover Illustration by Selma Waldman
Book Design: Jonathan Gullery

Library of Congress Cataloging-in-Publication Data

Pegram, Amelia Blossom
     Echoes across a thousand hills : poems / by Amelia Blossom Pegram.
       p.   cm.
     ISBN 0-86543-417-4 (HB). -- ISBN 0-86543-418-2 (PB)
     1. Mothers and daughters -- United States -- Poetry. 2. South African Americans -- Poetry. 3. Afro-American women -- Poetry. I. Title.
PS3566.E314E24   1994
811'.54--dc20   94-32021
                                           CIP

CONTENTS

ONE

TWO

THREE

FOUR

FIVE

SIX

SEVEN

EIGHT

NINE

TEN

Dedicated to my
daughter, Melanie Jean House
godchild, Colette Bosman
mentor, Leon Driskell

FOREWORD

Poet **Amelia Blossom Pegram**'s works have been influenced by her experiences of more than thirty years of living in England and the United States, far from her native Cape Town. She has worked as an actress, writer and teacher

And yet, in spite of her intimate acquaintance with life in these two countries in the course of her sojourn, *Echoes Across a Thousand Hills* strongly retains her view of life through African eyes.

The poet here speaks of universal themes: womanhood, love, and freedom. Her poetry is immediate, and aural. The pieces tend to be short, perhaps because she often performs the poetry. At her recitations the rapt attention of the audience is sustained throughout the length of her poems, In developing one idea, one concept, the poet carries her audience with her from start to finish.

Thirty years of living away from the land of one's birth can bring about a great transformation, The changes usually include taking on some of the characteristics of the natives of the adopted country and, oftentimes, fondness for the new land. Since hers was an involuntary emigration, the poet's emotional ties to South Africa are unsevered. In some of the poems she makes a clear distinction between rootlessness of exile and the rootedness of 'home.'

As a world traveller and native of South Africa, a multicultural land, Amelia Blossom Pegram has spoken at other times of her startling discovery of the widespread tendency to view the vast African continent as a "country." She hints at this vastness and diversity by her use of six southern African languages as well as Arabic, in the poem RETURN.

Selma Waldman who has contributed the visual responses, is well-known as an activist in the Anti-Apartheid movement. This is not their first collaboration. Artist and Poet have worked together on a number of projects.

During these days of change in South Africa, with more to come, these timely poems offer much to reflect upon. Reading this volume we are reminded that there is hope for a better future.

Esther Hall Mumford
Seattle, Washington

ACKNOWLEDGMENTS

One does not make this journey alone on an "express train." There are always many stops. I have been helped and supported every mile of the way.

Some poems were previously published in *Our Sun Will Rise, The Dark Woods I Cross, Say That me River Turns, Thinker Review, Essence* and *Drum Voices.*

Marilyn Durham, Anne Campbell, Donna Watson, and Nan Spalding listened and responded.

Velekaya Nongauza prevailed upon his colleagues at the United Nations for translations of *Return.*

David Knight willingly gave of his technological expertise.

My siblings, Owen, Naomi and Maud keep my feet firmly on the ground - rootedness.

Rashidah Ismaili, Sathima Bea Benjamin, Thelma Ravell-Pinto, Cecil Abrahams and Kereopetse Kgositsile retain the songs of Africa in me. Earline Valentine, Pat Taylor, Esther Mumford, and Bani Bennett taught me how to sing in new tones. Earbie Johnson and Horace Bond keep the music going. Earbie's drums speak the tongues of Africa.

I was also strengthened by the memories I have of my Mother and Father, Granny West, Aunty Maud and Uncle Chris.

ONE

RETURN

I've left my heart
on other continents
but
I have my home
on only one
I yearn to return
claim my place
in
Africa's sun.

BUYA!

Intliziyo yam ndihamba ndiyishi ya
kwezinye izithabakazi
kodwa ke
lkhaya lam likwesinye kuphela
Ndininqwenela ukubuya
Ndithathe ndibange indawo yam
Elangeni lase Afrika.

(Xhosa translation by Velekaya Nongauza)

BUYA

Ngishiye inhliziyo yami kwamanye
amazwekazi,
kodwa,
Nginekhaya kwelilodwa vo,
Ngilangazelela ukubuya ngithathe
isikhundla sami,
Phansi kwelanga le-Afrika.

(Zulu translation by Derrick Sipho Nbatha)

Inhlitiyo yami ngayishiya
Ngesheya emaveni
Keja
Nginelikhaya
Kulelinye live
Ngikhanuka kubuela emuva
Ngitsatsi indzawo yami
Phasi kwelilanga
Lase - Afrika

(SiSwati translation by Sibongile Nazibuko)

Pelo ea ka e setse matsekela
linaheng tsa sets'abelo,
Empa ke na le lehae le le leng le mofuthu
leo ke labalabelang hoboela ho lona
lona ke Afrika

(Sotho translation by Morongoenyane Mapheleba)

Nimenacha moye wangu
kwenye bara nyingine
Lakini
nina kwetu
Katika bara moja tu
Nini shanku kubwa ya kurejea
kuchukna nafasi yangu
katika
Jua la Afrika

(Kiswahili translation by Said G. Bilal)

Ke tlogetse pelo ya ka hwa
mafatsheng a mangwe
mme
Ke na le legae kwa go le lengwe
fela
Ke tlhoapaletse go bowa go
tsaya bonno ba me
kwa
Letsatsing la Afrika

(Setswana translation by Pule Leinaeng)

عـــودة

تركت فؤادي
في قارات أخرى
لكن
بيتي موجود
في قارة واحدة
أتوق إلى العودة
أطلب بنصيبي
من
شمس افريقيا

(Arabic translation by "Ahmed")

4

TWO

EVELYN

Mother,
guiding light
of my growing
shining through
my dark
and
happy days
glowing past
tears
and laughter
your spirit, lingers
in the circle
of my life-glow
to guide me still.

Mother,
In celebration
of your life
In thanksgiving
for the memories
a candle burns.

SARAH

Granny's smoke grey eyes
could see
far
past time
through walls
and me
even when I moved slowly
downstairs
avoiding
the creaky third step
Granny called out from her room
"Get back to bed now, child.
Just because you're quiet
don't mean I can't see you."
I'd go back to my room
to read under the covers.
"Put that book away.
Turn off that flashlight.
You'll spoil your eyes."
Granny could see through
walls and blankets
and
me.

QUEENMOTHER

you should have known
Mommy
fresh-starched aproned
head crowned with
tight braids
on Saturdays
reigning
in the kitchen
creating
golden crusty loaves
Sunday tea-cakes
apricot-jam-layered
coconut decorated
our Saturday Mommy
shelling peas
stringing beans
scraping carrots
chopping slaw
roasting potatoes & leg o' lamb
inviting our appetites
when only our noses
were allowed
on this sixth day
Mommy labored
for there was no
working
except
praying
hard
above the sisters & brothers
at the Baptist Mission
on the Lord's Day
we "Amened"
&
"Praised the Lord"

"Gave thanks"
for this day's
daily bread
peas/beans/carrots/potatoes lamb/&/jamcake
"Praise the Lord"
"Thy will be done on Earth"
Saturdays
by Mommy
You should have known
her.

MOTHER OF POETS

Gwendolyn - lady of new vision
I have heard
your voice
clear
rising at the dawning
sings the lark
sings the lark
Mother of Poets
I have seen
your fearless protection
of the young
jealously guarding
their fragile futures
nurturing new voices
to rise against the noon sky
sings the lark, sings the lark,
First lady of our visions
you have taught
our souls to sing
freedom
against the setting sun
sings the lark.

(for Gwendolyn Brooks)

NONTSIKELELO'S SONG

I will wipe my tears
and sing
tula tula
do not cry
for husband
and children
my heart
hold on to the dream
freedom
resist sharp
baton charges
trampling boots
softly sing
tula tula
do not scream
our children's pain
across saracened cities
be still my heart
guide my hands
to catch each gentle life
enfold our strong future
new blessings in my arms
to sing
tula tula tula.

(for Albertina Sisulu)

WINNIE

Sparrow against the wind
she flew
four forward
three back
buffeted
tossed on the currents
she flew
into the wind
persevering
to the goal
brave bird
flapping
through the storms
Sparrow against the wind.

(for Nomzamo Mandela)

MOTHER LEAH

weary of
L ipservice lament for South Africa
E mpty-eyed children waiting
A bandoned through live-in dreams
H opes shattered on Soweto streets

LEAH, Mother of Africa
weary of weariness
of the fight for the soil
of raising voices of defiance
with the soul of SADWA
weary of movement against rebirth

MOTHER LEAH

teaching new songs of praise
new hopes and fights
for family-embraced children
in free Soweto sunshine

(for Leah Tutu)

SADWA - South African Domestic Workers' Association

STARCHILD

sound
weaver
beyond the sparkling
cliched stars
cutting word facets
of diamond brilliance
shining
through enshrouding darkness
to highlight
woven webs
guiding non-seers
across cosmic chasms
to understand their ultimate being
through nothingness
into universal constellations.

(for Estella Conwill Majozo)

THREE

18

MELANIE

Child of darkness
   born
into the light
you must keep
   burning
to help in the
   struggle
to make
blackness
   right.

BIRTHING

I thought I heard
the bleating lamb
But
It was the cry
of my new offering
to the world,
I thought I heard
the bleating lamb
But
At your birth
My daughter
It was your cry
For my pain
And for
your births
To come.

NOTHING NEW UNDER THE SUN

i smiled
as my daughter
slanged
with her friends
thinking
i did not
understand
and remembered
how
my mother
smiled
as i coded
with my friends
thinking
she
did not understand.

CREATIONS

My daughter
You who have seen the rainbow
Have stood under the brilliance
twofold
You who have felt the rains
sweet and bitter
hold onto the colors
Colors you have touched
and spread
Poetry and stories
Performing
Your creations
Hold on
You who have seen the free
Unicorn
Under your rainbow
Hold fast
In our special way and time
We will always laugh
And dance together
Knowing we have been
under the bright double bows
Our rainbows.

MOONFLOW

when lambs chase
across new grass
with foals and calves
you weave
black-eyed daisies
in your braids
wrap around
gold-bead-embroidered
red skirt
join the women
at sunset
in the oval
to dance around the fire
where long lingering rays
steal through the branches
to join the flitting fireglow
in the twilight
you curtsy
with flowers
for each woman
until
The Old One
regales you, Our Daughter,
in anklets necklaces bracelets
generations old
as you greet the rising moon
whose flow you now know
our New Woman.

LULLABY

scared of the night
afraid of my eyelids trapped dark
lull me to sleep, Mommy
i cried
cried for the waking remained
my fevered head unable to nestle
on my lumpy pillow
rock me to sleep, Mommy,
i whispered
your mothsoft strokes
on my hair
my cheeks
gently kept time to your hushed
"Guten Abend, Guten Nacht"
my burning brow
athrob
"Morgen fruh"
seemed
far away.

SPACES

no bookbags
  shoes
      papers
         jackets
folders   socks
trail your path
through the house
neat square-set rugs
spaces unfilled
mark your absence
cabinets
  toothpaste
     closets
never left unshut
kitchen sinks empty
of unwashed dishes
after midnight snacks
spaces you left
grateful
dead silence
fills your room
no late night
early morning
telephone rings
disturb
i fill the silence
screaming
in those neat rooms
re-membering your presence
until semester break.

(for Melanie 1992)

25th DECEMBER, 1992

How shall I help
My Daughter,
you wait
like a sprinter
in the starting box
tense expectant
ready for the jump
the telephone bell
your father's voice
Christmas good wishes
connecting years
What can I say
My Daughter,
you wait
a hurt bird
nervous
ready to fly
if the mailman rings
your father's gift
hoped for connections
you wait
for remembered love
How shall I help?

FOUR

CYCLE

please, teacher,
my question is quite simple.
If the sun drinks
from the land
to fluff
the clouds
And the clouds
spill drops
on us below,
With all the
puddles
in South Africa
fresh splashed blood,
teacher,
Will the rain be red?

CHILDHOOD UNTOLD

my child,
one day
you will
hold
flowers
freely
strew
soft-colored petals
to cascade
around the head
of your love.
Now for freedoms love
you will
throw
the hard-silver
pineapple
to explode
the heart
of oppression.

ALMS

children of my country
for you
i weep
tattered balloon-bellied
hands cupped
beside the snaking
railway line
children
waiting for shed skins
begging scraps
from flashing travellers
your silent eyes
grown old
with mirthless hunger
children of South Africa
my tears
dried behind my eyes
for you.

BURIALS

dear God,
i didn't kill the butterfly
i only buried it
in the foilwrapped matchbox
because
i wanted it still to be pretty
for you
i sang one hymn
cried a little
i tend the grave
i found the dead sparrow
i buried it
in red crepewrapped shoebox
"All things bright and beautiful"
i sang again
but
dear God,
it's not because i loved burials
i don't need
five or ten daily
i don't know
what to sing
those children of Dimbaza had no time to be
bright and beautiful
i have run out of hymns
i cannot cry all day.

LEOPARD

I am here
beautiful strong child
glistening ebony
future of my people
man-child
and
don't call
me, boy.
that might stick
too hard to your tongue
stay forever, no boy,
I am here
strong glowing
black man-child
born to ride
the swift leopard
in survival
future of my people.

II.
I am here
to run with
the swift glowing
leopard
strong beautiful
ebony man-child
hope of my people
I am here
to survive
with the varied colored
leopard
soft steel
stretching

(for 6 yr. old Michael)

DIRGE

D R U M
for the dance
of new children of Africa
Drummm
Children
born as mothers
squat
on city sidewalks
Children
growing thin
their highlife
nightclub trashcans
D r u m
for the dance
DRUMMM
for the song
of new children of Africa
D r u m
Children
born
as mothers labor
in country
reddust
Children growing thin
feeding on lizards
death's
messengers
Drummm
for the song
mmm...

TRUANT

He stayed from school today
bad Billy bad
boys of eight
don't protest
South Africa's laws
bad bad Billy
don't call names
don't throw
sticks and stones
break policemen's bones
bad Billy bad
policemen beat with sticks
throw gas
bullets tearing
in the back
dead Billy dead.

(For the children of Cape Town)

FIVE

LIBATION

in spring's cool evening
i trail my fingers
across your surface
rippling
like a gentle breeze
over a lake
you rise and roll
to foam-tipped waves
breaking
on the shore.

VOWS

under cathedral arched branches
we knelt
in goldred leaves
spoke promises
tumbling words
uttering eternal love
now
walking through
redbrown leaves
renewing
vows
in wordwrapped
silence.

CROWNING

this fire
promise of
emeralds sapphires rubies
dancing
among stars
shining
through moonlight
across
our rolling flesh
this promise of fire
rainbow diamoned
light strobing
our rhythm
in fiery opals
flaming
our passion.

LIZO'S CRY

Man,
i will drink your tears
as you comfort
on my bosom
from the steel-sharp
childpain
you brought
your mother's
slow climb
alone
to the mountaintop
Manchild,
i will cradle
your torment
in the cavern
of my being
enfold
your loneliness
in my warmth.

THREADS

i need to have you
at my center
web
each fiber of your being
out
into the reaches
of my
understanding
of your youness
i need to center
you
in my web
draw each thread
out beyond
the narrow confines
of your body
to the meeting
of souls.

TRYST

tonight
soft and warm
i wait my turn
great Nile-River-fluid
   brownbody flow
you'll come
dip in my waters
let the night air
echo   echo
your singing thighs
roll in the heat of my mud
   surround you
stop daybreak
tomorrow
day-clean
the music stops
   the air stills
i carry my waters
to the sea.

DRUMMER

My mama said
"Watch the drum. Watch the drum."
I watched
watched the drum
I did I did
Saw swollen steel-hooped belly
skin stretched smooth top
I waited
"What's to watch, mama?"
"Watch the drum..er. drum..er" Mama said
The drum..er drum..er er er
I heard its heart
Flesh vibrating sound
Saw the drummer
Gone to the beat
Flesh on flesh
Pulsing through me
Feet tingling sound
Mama said, "Watch the drum"
I joined the drum..er drum..er mm drummer
vibrated flesh on flesh
er er

SIX

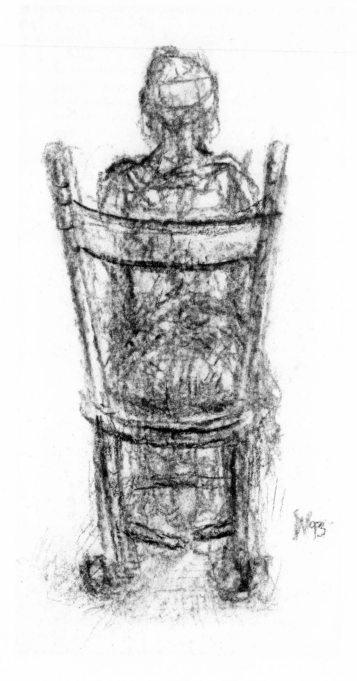

MADONNA OR RITUAL AT THE CAPE OF GOOD HOPE

We skipped our circle of laughter
around her.
This nameless woman gaunt as a winter tree
"Lady, Lady, let' see your baby!"
"Looks just like his Father!"
we nudged each other
tightening our circle
around her hunched body.
She sat on her porch
rocking her fantasy
last year's Nativity Pageant Jesus
in her arms
held together by threadbare sleeves.
"Lady, Lady, let's see your baby!"
We knew only of babies
dried on shrivelled-prune breasts
her children dropped like green fruit
from a sapless tree.
All she knew
was locked behind her stare
vacant of living.
All we knew we circled
around her in our laughter.

SISTERSONG

Are you singing sister?
the song's the same.
Sing it softly
rocking
baby
Sing it swiftly
cooking
dinner
Sing it wildly
making
love
Sing it harshly
pounding
corn
Sing it loudly
washing
clothes
Are you singing, sister?
The song's the same
You carry the melody
not
the licks
for you
the song
is always
the same.

WOMANSPEAK

tearing my skirts
jumping the hedgerows
racing barefoot through
the brush
ribboned ponytails flapping in the chase
swinging exhausted through the gate
flopping on the porch
to catch a breath

Those were girl-days

Now I have tamed my hair
closecrop
Thirty-six ceed my breasts
Ensheathed hips in pencil-slim skirt
Step sedate
feet imprisoned
in stiletto pumps

And you come by say
Girl, looking mighty fine.
What's happening, Girl?

Five-foot-two frame stretched tall
I heave my breasts
toss my head
"Did I hear you call me, GIRL?"

ON THE OLD BANJO

dum dum dee dee dum dum
dee dee dum

if you know this song
women
sing dum dee dee dum

in the light of the sky
men perform the eagles soar
our wings are strong
despite their clipping
through this glass ceiling
we will rise above
their bidding

dum dum dee dee dum
if you know this song
sisters
sing dum dee dee dum

promotion denied
too short too tall
too lean too fat
too butch too feminine
and all that
pms pregnancy childcare stuff
too woman

dum dum dum dee
if you know this song
mothers
sing dee dee dum dum

custodial parent
outside the fathers play-round
you dance with the future
dum dum dum
you are the music
and the monkey

dum dum dee dee dum
dum.

MOTHER'S GARDEN

in morning's first dew
you entered my garden
grew tall
one black rose
tenderly nurtured
through
noon's abusive sun
drought's neglect
in the afternoon's warmth
you stretched skyward
strongly
now
in evening's cool breeze
your
velvet black petals
unfold
for the pluckers pleasure.

SISTERCALL

you don't have to
perpetuate their myth
my brothers
don't have to be
no superstud
don't have to prove
no manhood
on their bedhopping terms
so they be locking up their women
because your manhood oozes
thru cracks
they say
you don't have to
perpetuate
their myth
my brothers
it's okay to love one woman
come in pleasure with her
just hold her close
share your pain
don't have to prove
no manhood
if you be men
my brothers.

MOTHERSONG

with song
grown old
mightily
stopping
the red flow
of the moon
for new
fruit
along
the lifebearing Nile
Be I not woman?
Wonderfully so?

grown old
in the dance
with sagging breasts
sucked dry
for young warriors
of the pulsing
rhythmic Niger
Woman I be
Uniquely so.

SEVEN

HE LOVES ME . . .

depetalled flower
cupped in hand
that summer
i waited
on the hillside
beneath our engraved tree
blew the yellow dust
to join the white petals
in the breeze
to reach him
in redstained green jungle
where on starless nights
he shot down
movement
for freedom
he waited on defoliaged hillside
in orange sunset
to disperse for my safety
the red peril
but he did not return
to see me pluck petals
. . . he loves me not.

SEGMENTS

If I need an "as" or a "like"
to shape a poem
of our marriage
let it be a grapefruit
After I have discarded
the bitter rind
of my anger and regret
I bite into the
memories meat
bitter sour sweet
our flesh on the
bones of our daughter
your smile in her eyes
of brighter times
sour the juice
trickling with the
sucking of each segment
of our marriage
bitter
your inability to
slake your lust
on the grapefruit.

SYNCHRONIZATION

Too late I understood
your silence
was not a refusal
of the dance
but the getting in
touch with the rhythm
feeling the beat
of the drum
Too late I understood
your hesitation
was not a denial
But like a surfer
you waited for the big wave
hovered only to catch
the upbeat
your entry to the dance
Through your silence
I moved alone
shaking your refusal
through my body in the dance
watched you swept into
the rhythm of another
Too late I understood
your silent hovering
was a pause for - perfection.

NIGHTFALL

as purple shades
usher in the night
i lock myself
in our room
darkly hemmed in by
memories
we almost shared
in the pressing darkness
i reach out
to pull the purple nightshade
as comforter around me
no longer taunted
i submit.

CODA

when tenderness is gone
the lightest touch
pains
the softest whisper
screeches the air
the faintest smells
weigh the morning dew
the most delicate taste
cloys
the prettiest picture
sours
when tenderness is gone
farewells remain.

PROMISES

blanketed
in warm summer nights
beneath the shady elms
on the lush blue-grass slopes
under the orange
July moon
you assured
me of your love
promised eternity
Now by stark naked trees
in icebound hills
under steel-blue
January moon
i wait
without promised love
to wrap
in cold winter nights.

SPACES TO FILL

your departure
marked by no note for me
only empty
closets
spaces on the bookshelves
no music
there should have been
music
songs for the dance
your departure
left no reason
only
my arms empty
my stares unable
to will you back
you left
the toilet seat up
dripped pomade and hairs
in the sink
your cologne and aftershave
scenting through the house
the dent in your pillow
a void in my life
and
the pain of it
if
when you find yourself
know
you have spaces to refill.

EIGHT

REBIRTH

she sat in a corner
hunched
through the lashing
inside her memory
members
of her remembering
pieces of herself
circling
through the darkness
into the inner caverns of
herselfness
slowly
she rose
to find
the sun her warming warning
return
her pieces
re-membered
herself restored
viewed in the light
of a new
dawning
whole beginnings.

FORMATION

swirling
from beyond nothingness
through time
and space
spiralling
words
The Poet
She
collects within herself
gestation of poems
to bear
down
in rhythmic measure
across
the naked page.

REVELATION

from the mud
of ancient
rivers
i have molded
my face
Now through my mask generations old
I feel your
hands cup my face
as you
gently peel away
antique layers
Uncertainly
anticipate
the moment
you draw nearer
Or repel
my naked image

S/HE BLUES

drum
drum drum
drum me drum
me drum
drum me?
no!
Skin-tight air
me?
no.
me no drum.
Drum me no drum
drum.

BUTTERFLY

once again
vulnerable
she folded
her wings
together
silently
sat suspended
dreading
the danger
of capture
and
mount.

WORDPOWER

Granny needed
no dictionary
said she never
used
a word of no meaning
to her
she always had folks
explain
themselves
real plain
she never used
superfluous
words
even that one was
wasted breath
Granny said
words were for sound
pleasure
to touch others
in sadness
or
joy.

FIXED

cats
hip in alleys
howl
crank
songs
screech
across
snow
leap
high
crack
glass
ear-splitting
distress.

PRAYER

comfort oh comfort
comfort
women
battling
warrior invasions
of fragile bodies
comfort
comfort oh comfort
mothers
suffering
soldier incisions
for delicate babies
comfort oh comfort
women
fighting
marauder snatches
from starving children
oh comfort
mothers
protesting
police harassments
of underprivileged youth
comfort comfort
women
of Japan and Somalia
mothers
of Bosnia and the U.S.A.
comfort oh comfort.

NINE

NUPTIAL PRAYER

Dear God,
As we greet this new day,
Beginning of our new life,
Help us to grow
in understanding
of our individual uniqueness
so that our love
will not demand
conformity,
will allow criticism without insult
will allow and respect
our personal growth.

As we open our hearts
to your guidance,
Lead us to end each day
in love
not anger and misunderstanding
let us be open
to each other
to talk our pain
talk our joy
Have no exclusions
Lead us to
pray our hurting
pray our celebration

In our fresh sunshine
Let us see the beauty
of the rose
not linger on the thorns
See beyond the death
of seeds and caterpillars
to the wonder of flowers
and butterflies

In your mercy, Lord,
Help us to keep faithful
In this journey of life
Amen

(for Nicki and Steve)

MATTHEW 25:42-43

Dear Lord
I had so much
cleaning to do
Had to clear my closets
of has-been styles
Couldn't be seen
out of fashion
for this year's season
Lord, I was so busy
Got those clothes bagged
Put them in the alley.
The barely-clad beggar
got them first.
He is strangely scarred
haunting marks across his forehead
eyes staring
piercing,
Dear Lord,
I had so much
cleaning
defrost the fridge
sort out the larder
dishes to clean
so much left-over food
to trash.
The awkward alley-cat child
got the bagged food.
He gulped it down
thin fingers darting
from trashbag to mouth
Dear Lord,
Why do the naked and hungry
nuisance the alley of my life?

ASSURANCE

as the tornado wrecks
havoc around me
i will find my refuge
in the center of the storm
as the storm waves
crash around me
i will find my peace
in the depths of the ocean
as the earth shakes
the mountains and valleys
i will find my shelter
in the core of the earth
My Christ will penetrate
the center of storms
the depths of oceans
the core of the earth
to keep my spirit safe
above the present living
of my life.

PASSIONBLUES

if the blues be
sorrow pain and joy
Then my Jesus
He knew the blues

giving all
His life of love
all his love for life
then by friends
denied betrayed
Yes, my Jesus
He knew the blues

crowned in thorns
spat upon
then crucified
drank the bitter
cup of pain
The blues
my Jesus
He knew the blues

died upon a cross
He did
watched in scorn
by hungry mobs
buried in a tomb
He was
shut behind the
heavy rock
Yes, the blues
my Jesus knew

Rose triumphant
on Easter morn

His blood and flesh
our only grace
my Jesus
He beat the blues.

SEEMING

and wingless flight
my soul needs now
to soar
within
above
to lift
my spirits through the day
to see beyond
the dying petals
of the rose
to seek
the flower
in the dungheap
to see beyond
the death
of seed
and caterpillar
to the flower and butterfly
my soul
needs now
to soar
above
the seeming of my life.

WILLOW

dance in the wind
  long skirts
on water
dancing in the wind
skirts sweeping water
  green frills
swaying
to the violins
  in your hair
     dance
         in
             the
                 wind.

FALL

i always like Fall
best
smoke meat
barbecue
end of season corn
baked apples
crackling sugar and raisins
and fresh coleslaw
to eat
we sit on the porch
watching the sky colors
match the trees
no mosquitoes
no humidity
and we sleep with open windows
after a day
jumping in piles of leaves
golden brown.

HYDE PARK

Winter turns the beds
top side down
to boast for months
her fresh
white linen,
Overnight
Spring sheds the white sheets
to sport her flowered
patch work quilt.

A RAIN POEM FOR DAWN

i will dance with the flowers
to the beat
of the raindrops
at my feet
i will sing with the rivers
to the tune
of the raindrops
on the hills.

TEN

N'DIZOBUYA

imprisoned
from Seattle to Louisville
in the belly of the silver bird
i peek from
a tiny orifice
through the white-whipped layers
across
rolling mountains
snaking rivers
lost oxbows
silent lakes
patched greenbrown plains
and see
across Atlantic Ocean
Cape Peninsula
through whispy-white clothed
Table Mountain
to a distant
homecoming.

POLYRHYTHMS

after
the heat
boots
billyclubs
you swing
electrodes
scrunched
cries of pain
you hear
cries of surrender
your victory
but
through the circle
of fire
i hear
aching songs
defiant spirits
heralding
dances
of triumph.

THE INTERVIEW

I heard the question, man.
Let me hear it out loud, for you.
You asked,
"When will your freedom struggle be over?"
"Right?"
I say the name is
Liberation
did you get that? Dig?
Your question begs a new label
for my cause
or a restatement
a new emphasis
to appease your weariness.
Listen
I heard your question.
No, it is not
free to struggle
the end is not the journey
Let me repeat
Strive to be free.
Liberation
is the word.
You dig?

Do we move on to the next question?

MEMORY

remember
i need not have your shadow
on paper
our spirits met and touched
many times before we see
each other again
we will sing
we will dance
with the drum
as our spirits meet
Would it matter
if your face
i no longer
could remember?

DRUMPULSE

with my fathers' drum
pulsating through me
i raced with the feet
of a gazelle
to dance with the wind
across the plains.
with my fathers' drum
vibrating in me
i swayed with the grace
of a giraffe
to dance with the rain
across the hills

HOMAGE

removed
from missionary processions
we dance
around distant fires
sing
love honor victory
to ancient drums
counter-tuned
to gregorian chants.
circling far-off fires
we venerate
ancestors
songs
rising through
drum spirits.

MARTIN LUTHER KING JR.

Martin, named for war
You soared in peace
above the hatred
Flying high
to seek a freedom
Not as a slave in death
But as a man
Free at last
to know that
Change was gonna come
Martin, man of peace
Your spirit
moves
to seek out truth
Beyond the memory
of your songs
To a free man's cry
Free at last.

LIBERATION

Birth
Blood
Afterbirth
Blood
Purification
Freedom
Celebration

ECHOES

in loud reverberations
across verdant valleys
of a thousand hills
dancing to the drum
not whispered through cracks
in secret caves
my voice celebrates
the poetry
of the ancestral word
in joyful song
over gray concrete cities
not choked in sterile pages
my voice resounds
the music
of my ancestors' words.

FIRECIRCLE

Out of your fiery womb
We danced
Circled reddust
   against the dawn
Our feet branded the soil
Now we arise
through the pain of dispossession
Splashing our blood
   against the noonsun
Till we arrive
At the victors' circle
Arms raised, faces lifted
Soil reclaimed
To
Dance the red dust
   against the sunset.

UMBHIYOZO

Let the drum
sing
UMBHIYOZO

Even now as then
We color our words
To the stroke of the drum
To the drum
We color our words

From the yellow glow of dawning
to the golden blaze of sunset
we pace our dance
to the beat of the drum
celebrating
the rich yield
of our free land
we color our words
GOLD

And the drum sings
UMBHIYOZO

As the drum vibrates
across green hills
green valleys
we dance on plains with fresh
hopes of lush harvest
the drum sounds the call
GREEN
we color our words
Green

The ancient drum
speaks the rhythm of Africa

from beyond time
Power
the color
BLACK
proud heritage
the strength to overcome
the pain
the strength
to regain
BLACK

the drum's tremble
echoes
across a thousand hills
Umbhiyozo Umbhiyozo

We color our words
in the echoes
of the drum
GOLD GREEN BLACK
UMBHIYOZO.

AMELIA BLOSSOM PEGRAM studied at the University of Cape Town, the Guildhall School of Music and Drama, the University of Leeds, and the University of Louisville. She has internationally published poems, short stories, critical essays, book reviews, and theater criticism. Her work has been translated into several languages. Her dramatic works include *You've Struck a Rock* performed at the Kentucky Center for the Arts, and a collaboration on the widely performed and *The Dance Goes On*. She has performed professionally in film, radio and stage.

SELMA WALDMAN completed studies in Berlin on a Fulbright grant. Her works are in the permanent collections of the Berlin Museum, Judische Abteilung, the memorial Terezin Ghetto Museum (The Czech Republic), the Judah L. Magnes Museum (Berkeley, California), the National Museum of Women in the Arts (Washington, DC), and various museums in the Southwest. Drawings of a progressive and feminist nature and for human rights causes, works documenting liberation movements and political prisoners, works exploring the effects of apartheid and war have been published in the U.S.A., Europe, Canada, India, Africa and the Mideast. Waldman lives and teaches in Seattle, Washington.